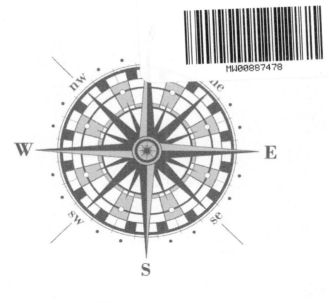

Travel is Fatal To Prejudice, Bigotry and Narrow-Mindedness

- Marc Twain -

From / To: ....

GPS Coordinates: .... Miles Traveled: ....

Campground: ....

Address: ....

Site: ....

Check in: .... Check out: .... Cost: ....

☐ Water	☐ Easy Access	☆☆☆☆☆	Location
☐ Sewer	☐ Paved	☆☆☆☆☆	Amenities
☐ Electricity	☐ Restrooms	☆☆☆☆☆	Cleanliness
☐ Wfi	☐ Laundry	☆☆☆☆☆	Security
☐ Fire Ring	☐ Store / Cafe	☆☆☆☆☆	Overall

Pros / Cons: ....

....

....

Notes: ....

....

....

....

....

....

....

....

From / To:

GPS Coordinates: _____ Miles Traveled: _____

Campground: _____

Address: _____

Site: _____

Check in: _____ Check out: _____ Cost: _____

☐ Water	☐ Easy Access	☆☆☆☆☆ Location
☐ Sewer	☐ Paved	☆☆☆☆☆ Amenities
☐ Electricity	☐ Restrooms	☆☆☆☆☆ Cleanliness
☐ Wfi	☐ Laundry	☆☆☆☆☆ Security
☐ Fire Ring	☐ Store / Cafe	☆☆☆☆☆ Overall

Pros / Cons: _____

Notes: _____

From / To: ....

GPS Coordinates: .... Miles Traveled: ....

Campground: ....

Address: ....

Site: ....

Check in: .... Check out: .... Cost: ....

☐ Water	☐ Easy Access	☆☆☆☆☆ Location
☐ Sewer	☐ Paved	☆☆☆☆☆ Amenities
☐ Electricity	☐ Restrooms	☆☆☆☆☆ Cleanliness
☐ Wfi	☐ Laundry	☆☆☆☆☆ Security
☐ Fire Ring	☐ Store / Cafe	☆☆☆☆☆ Overall

Pros / Cons: ....

....

....

Notes: ....

....

....

....

....

....

....

....

From / To:..

GPS Coordinates:.. Miles Traveled:......................

Campground:..

Address:..

Site:..

Check in:............................. Check out:............................. Cost:.....................

☐ Water	☐ Easy Access	☆☆☆☆☆ Location
☐ Sewer	☐ Paved	☆☆☆☆☆ Amenities
☐ Electricity	☐ Restrooms	☆☆☆☆☆ Cleanliness
☐ Wfi	☐ Laundry	☆☆☆☆☆ Security
☐ Fire Ring	☐ Store / Cafe	☆☆☆☆☆ Overall

Pros / Cons:...

Notes:...

From / To:_____

GPS Coordinates:_____ Miles Traveled:_____

Campground:_____

Address:_____

Site:_____

Check in:_____ Check out:_____ Cost:_____

☐ Water	☐ Easy Access	☆☆☆☆☆ Location
☐ Sewer	☐ Paved	☆☆☆☆☆ Amenities
☐ Electricity	☐ Restrooms	☆☆☆☆☆ Cleanliness
☐ Wfi	☐ Laundry	☆☆☆☆☆ Security
☐ Fire Ring	☐ Store / Cafe	☆☆☆☆☆ Overall

Pros / Cons:_____

_____

_____

Notes:_____

_____

_____

_____

_____

_____

_____

_____

From / To:..

GPS Coordinates:.. Miles Traveled:..........................

Campground:..

Address:..

Site:..

Check in:........................... Check out:........................... Cost:...........................

☐ Water   ☐ Easy Access   ☆☆☆☆☆ Location

☐ Sewer   ☐ Paved   ☆☆☆☆☆ Amenities

☐ Electricity   ☐ Restrooms   ☆☆☆☆☆ Cleanliness

☐ Wfi   ☐ Laundry   ☆☆☆☆☆ Security

☐ Fire Ring   ☐ Store / Cafe   ☆☆☆☆☆ Overall

Pros / Cons:..

_____

_____

Notes:..

_____

_____

_____

_____

_____

_____

_____

From / To:..

GPS Coordinates:.. Miles Traveled:......................

Campground:...

Address:..

Site:..

Check in:.......................... Check out:.......................... Cost:..........................

☐ Water	☐ Easy Access	☆☆☆☆☆ Location
☐ Sewer	☐ Paved	☆☆☆☆☆ Amenities
☐ Electricity	☐ Restrooms	☆☆☆☆☆ Cleanliness
☐ Wfi	☐ Laundry	☆☆☆☆☆ Security
☐ Fire Ring	☐ Store / Cafe	☆☆☆☆☆ Overall

Pros / Cons:...

....

....

Notes:...

....

....

....

....

....

....

....

From / To:..

GPS Coordinates:..Miles Traveled:............................

Campground:..

Address:..

Site:...

Check in:.............................. Check out:.............................. Cost:..............................

☐ Water	☐ Easy Access	☆☆☆☆☆ Location
☐ Sewer	☐ Paved	☆☆☆☆☆ Amenities
☐ Electricity	☐ Restrooms	☆☆☆☆☆ Cleanliness
☐ Wfi	☐ Laundry	☆☆☆☆☆ Security
☐ Fire Ring	☐ Store / Cafe	☆☆☆☆☆ Overall

Pros / Cons:..

_____

_____

Notes:...

_____

_____

_____

_____

_____

_____

_____

From / To:_____

GPS Coordinates:_____ Miles Traveled:_____

Campground:_____

Address:_____

Site:_____

Check in:_____ Check out:_____ Cost:_____

☐ Water	☐ Easy Access	☆☆☆☆☆ Location
☐ Sewer	☐ Paved	☆☆☆☆☆ Amenities
☐ Electricity	☐ Restrooms	☆☆☆☆☆ Cleanliness
☐ Wfi	☐ Laundry	☆☆☆☆☆ Security
☐ Fire Ring	☐ Store / Cafe	☆☆☆☆☆ Overall

Pros / Cons:_____

_____

_____

Notes:_____

_____

_____

_____

_____

_____

_____

_____

From / To:

GPS Coordinates: _____ Miles Traveled: _____

Campground: _____

Address: _____

Site: _____

Check in: _____ Check out: _____ Cost: _____

☐ Water	☐ Easy Access	☆☆☆☆☆ Location
☐ Sewer	☐ Paved	☆☆☆☆☆ Amenities
☐ Electricity	☐ Restrooms	☆☆☆☆☆ Cleanliness
☐ Wfi	☐ Laundry	☆☆☆☆☆ Security
☐ Fire Ring	☐ Store / Cafe	☆☆☆☆☆ Overall

Pros / Cons: _____

_____

_____

Notes: _____

_____

_____

_____

_____

_____

_____

_____

_____

From / To:_____

GPS Coordinates:_____ Miles Traveled:_____

Campground:_____

Address:_____

Site:_____

Check in:_____ Check out:_____ Cost:_____

☐ Water	☐ Easy Access	☆☆☆☆☆ Location
☐ Sewer	☐ Paved	☆☆☆☆☆ Amenities
☐ Electricity	☐ Restrooms	☆☆☆☆☆ Cleanliness
☐ Wfi	☐ Laundry	☆☆☆☆☆ Security
☐ Fire Ring	☐ Store / Cafe	☆☆☆☆☆ Overall

Pros / Cons:_____

_____

_____

Notes:_____

_____

_____

_____

_____

_____

_____

_____

From / To: ....

GPS Coordinates: .... Miles Traveled: ....

Campground: ....

Address: ....

Site: ....

Check in: .... Check out: .... Cost: ....

☐ Water   ☐ Easy Access   ☆☆☆☆☆ Location

☐ Sewer   ☐ Paved   ☆☆☆☆☆ Amenities

☐ Electricity   ☐ Restrooms   ☆☆☆☆☆ Cleanliness

☐ Wfi   ☐ Laundry   ☆☆☆☆☆ Security

☐ Fire Ring   ☐ Store / Cafe   ☆☆☆☆☆ Overall

Pros / Cons: ....

....

....

Notes: ....

....

....

....

....

....

....

....

From / To:_____

GPS Coordinates:_____ Miles Traveled:_____

Campground:_____

Address:_____

Site:_____

Check in:_____ Check out:_____ Cost:_____

- ☐ Water
- ☐ Sewer
- ☐ Electricity
- ☐ Wfi
- ☐ Fire Ring

- ☐ Easy Access
- ☐ Paved
- ☐ Restrooms
- ☐ Laundry
- ☐ Store / Cafe

☆☆☆☆☆ Location

☆☆☆☆☆ Amenities

☆☆☆☆☆ Cleanliness

☆☆☆☆☆ Security

☆☆☆☆☆ Overall

Pros / Cons:_____

_____

_____

Notes:_____

_____

_____

_____

_____

_____

_____

_____

From / To:_____

GPS Coordinates:_____ Miles Traveled:_____

Campground:_____

Address:_____

Site:_____

Check in:_____ Check out:_____ Cost:_____

☐ Water	☐ Easy Access	☆☆☆☆☆ Location
☐ Sewer	☐ Paved	☆☆☆☆☆ Amenities
☐ Electricity	☐ Restrooms	☆☆☆☆☆ Cleanliness
☐ Wfi	☐ Laundry	☆☆☆☆☆ Security
☐ Fire Ring	☐ Store / Cafe	☆☆☆☆☆ Overall

Pros / Cons:_____

_____

_____

Notes:_____

_____

_____

_____

_____

_____

_____

_____

From / To: ....

GPS Coordinates: .... Miles Traveled: ....

Campground: ....

Address: ....

Site: ....

Check in: .... Check out: .... Cost: ....

☐ Water	☐ Easy Access	☆☆☆☆☆ Location
☐ Sewer	☐ Paved	☆☆☆☆☆ Amenities
☐ Electricity	☐ Restrooms	☆☆☆☆☆ Cleanliness
☐ Wfi	☐ Laundry	☆☆☆☆☆ Security
☐ Fire Ring	☐ Store / Cafe	☆☆☆☆☆ Overall

Pros / Cons: ....

....

....

Notes: ....

....

....

....

....

....

....

....

....

From / To:...

GPS Coordinates:.. Miles Traveled:................................

Campground:...

Address:...

Site:..

Check in:.. Check out:.. Cost:..............................

☐ Water   ☐ Easy Access   ☆ ☆ ☆ ☆ ☆ Location

☐ Sewer   ☐ Paved   ☆ ☆ ☆ ☆ ☆ Amenities

☐ Electricity   ☐ Restrooms   ☆ ☆ ☆ ☆ ☆ Cleanliness

☐ Wfi   ☐ Laundry   ☆ ☆ ☆ ☆ ☆ Security

☐ Fire Ring   ☐ Store / Cafe   ☆ ☆ ☆ ☆ ☆ Overall

Pros / Cons:...

_____

_____

Notes:..

_____

_____

_____

_____

_____

_____

_____

From / To:..

GPS Coordinates:.. Miles Traveled:..................

Campground:..

Address:..

Site:...

Check in:.......................... Check out:.......................... Cost:........................

☐ Water	☐ Easy Access	☆☆☆☆☆ Location
☐ Sewer	☐ Paved	☆☆☆☆☆ Amenities
☐ Electricity	☐ Restrooms	☆☆☆☆☆ Cleanliness
☐ Wfi	☐ Laundry	☆☆☆☆☆ Security
☐ Fire Ring	☐ Store / Cafe	☆☆☆☆☆ Overall

Pros / Cons:..

_____

_____

Notes:..

_____

_____

_____

_____

_____

_____

_____

From / To: ....

GPS Coordinates: .... Miles Traveled: ....

Campground: ....

Address: ....

Site: ....

Check in: .... Check out: .... Cost: ....

☐ Water	☐ Easy Access	☆☆☆☆☆ Location
☐ Sewer	☐ Paved	☆☆☆☆☆ Amenities
☐ Electricity	☐ Restrooms	☆☆☆☆☆ Cleanliness
☐ Wfi	☐ Laundry	☆☆☆☆☆ Security
☐ Fire Ring	☐ Store / Cafe	☆☆☆☆☆ Overall

Pros / Cons: ....

....

....

Notes: ....

....

....

....

....

....

....

....

....

From / To:...

GPS Coordinates:... Miles Traveled:...........................

Campground:...

Address:...

Site:..

Check in:............................. Check out:............................. Cost:...........................

☐ Water   ☐ Easy Access   ☆☆☆☆☆ Location

☐ Sewer   ☐ Paved   ☆☆☆☆☆ Amenities

☐ Electricity   ☐ Restrooms   ☆☆☆☆☆ Cleanliness

☐ Wfi   ☐ Laundry   ☆☆☆☆☆ Security

☐ Fire Ring   ☐ Store / Cafe   ☆☆☆☆☆ Overall

Pros / Cons:...

_____

_____

Notes:..

_____

_____

_____

_____

_____

_____

_____

From / To:

GPS Coordinates: Miles Traveled:

Campground:

Address:

Site:

Check in: Check out: Cost:

☐ Water	☐ Easy Access	☆☆☆☆☆ Location
☐ Sewer	☐ Paved	☆☆☆☆☆ Amenities
☐ Electricity	☐ Restrooms	☆☆☆☆☆ Cleanliness
☐ Wfi	☐ Laundry	☆☆☆☆☆ Security
☐ Fire Ring	☐ Store / Cafe	☆☆☆☆☆ Overall

Pros / Cons:

Notes:

From / To:..

GPS Coordinates:.. Miles Traveled:.........................

Campground:...

Address:...

Site:..

Check in:.............................. Check out:................................... Cost:.............................

☐ Water   ☐ Easy Access   ☆☆☆☆☆ Location

☐ Sewer   ☐ Paved   ☆☆☆☆☆ Amenities

☐ Electricity   ☐ Restrooms   ☆☆☆☆☆ Cleanliness

☐ Wfi   ☐ Laundry   ☆☆☆☆☆ Security

☐ Fire Ring   ☐ Store / Cafe   ☆☆☆☆☆ Overall

Pros / Cons:...

Notes:..

From / To:...

GPS Coordinates:..Miles Traveled:..................

Campground:...

Address:...

Site:...

Check in:.......................... Check out:..........................Cost:..............................

☐ Water	☐ Easy Access	☆☆☆☆☆ Location
☐ Sewer	☐ Paved	☆☆☆☆☆ Amenities
☐ Electricity	☐ Restrooms	☆☆☆☆☆ Cleanliness
☐ Wfi	☐ Laundry	☆☆☆☆☆ Security
☐ Fire Ring	☐ Store / Cafe	☆☆☆☆☆ Overall

Pros / Cons:..

_____

_____

Notes:..

_____

_____

_____

_____

_____

_____

_____

From / To: ....

GPS Coordinates: .... Miles Traveled: ....

Campground: ....

Address: ....

Site: ....

Check in: .... Check out: .... Cost: ....

☐ Water   ☐ Easy Access   ☆☆☆☆☆ Location

☐ Sewer   ☐ Paved   ☆☆☆☆☆ Amenities

☐ Electricity   ☐ Restrooms   ☆☆☆☆☆ Cleanliness

☐ Wfi   ☐ Laundry   ☆☆☆☆☆ Security

☐ Fire Ring   ☐ Store / Cafe   ☆☆☆☆☆ Overall

Pros / Cons: ....

....

....

Notes: ....

....

....

....

....

....

....

....

From / To:

GPS Coordinates: .... Miles Traveled: ....

Campground: ....

Address: ....

Site: ....

Check in: .... Check out: .... Cost: ....

☐ Water	☐ Easy Access	☆☆☆☆☆ Location
☐ Sewer	☐ Paved	☆☆☆☆☆ Amenities
☐ Electricity	☐ Restrooms	☆☆☆☆☆ Cleanliness
☐ Wfi	☐ Laundry	☆☆☆☆☆ Security
☐ Fire Ring	☐ Store / Cafe	☆☆☆☆☆ Overall

Pros / Cons:

Notes:

From / To:_____

GPS Coordinates:_____ Miles Traveled:_____

Campground:_____

Address:_____

Site:_____

Check in:_____ Check out:_____ Cost:_____

☐ Water	☐ Easy Access	☆☆☆☆☆ Location
☐ Sewer	☐ Paved	☆☆☆☆☆ Amenities
☐ Electricity	☐ Restrooms	☆☆☆☆☆ Cleanliness
☐ Wfi	☐ Laundry	☆☆☆☆☆ Security
☐ Fire Ring	☐ Store / Cafe	☆☆☆☆☆ Overall

Pros / Cons:_____

_____

_____

Notes:_____

_____

_____

_____

_____

_____

_____

_____

From / To:...

GPS Coordinates:... Miles Traveled:...............

Campground:..

Address:...

Site:..

Check in:............................. Check out:............................ Cost:...................

☐ Water	☐ Easy Access	☆☆☆☆☆ Location
☐ Sewer	☐ Paved	☆☆☆☆☆ Amenities
☐ Electricity	☐ Restrooms	☆☆☆☆☆ Cleanliness
☐ Wfi	☐ Laundry	☆☆☆☆☆ Security
☐ Fire Ring	☐ Store / Cafe	☆☆☆☆☆ Overall

Pros / Cons:...

Notes:...

From / To: ....

GPS Coordinates: .... Miles Traveled: ....

Campground: ....

Address: ....

Site: ....

Check in: .... Check out: .... Cost: ....

☐ Water   ☐ Easy Access   ☆☆☆☆☆ Location

☐ Sewer   ☐ Paved   ☆☆☆☆☆ Amenities

☐ Electricity   ☐ Restrooms   ☆☆☆☆☆ Cleanliness

☐ Wfi   ☐ Laundry   ☆☆☆☆☆ Security

☐ Fire Ring   ☐ Store / Cafe   ☆☆☆☆☆ Overall

Pros / Cons: ....

Notes: ....

From / To: ....

GPS Coordinates: .... Miles Traveled: ....

Campground: ....

Address: ....

Site: ....

Check in: .... Check out: .... Cost: ....

☐ Water   ☐ Easy Access   ☆☆☆☆☆ Location

☐ Sewer   ☐ Paved   ☆☆☆☆☆ Amenities

☐ Electricity   ☐ Restrooms   ☆☆☆☆☆ Cleanliness

☐ Wfi   ☐ Laundry   ☆☆☆☆☆ Security

☐ Fire Ring   ☐ Store / Cafe   ☆☆☆☆☆ Overall

Pros / Cons: ....

_____

_____

Notes: ....

_____

_____

_____

_____

_____

_____

_____

From / To:_____

GPS Coordinates:_____ Miles Traveled:_____

Campground:_____

Address:_____

Site:_____

Check in:_____ Check out:_____ Cost:_____

☐ Water   ☐ Easy Access   ☆☆☆☆☆   Location

☐ Sewer   ☐ Paved   ☆☆☆☆☆   Amenities

☐ Electricity   ☐ Restrooms   ☆☆☆☆☆   Cleanliness

☐ Wfi   ☐ Laundry   ☆☆☆☆☆   Security

☐ Fire Ring   ☐ Store / Cafe   ☆☆☆☆☆   Overall

Pros / Cons:_____

_____

_____

Notes:_____

_____

_____

_____

_____

_____

_____

_____

From / To:

GPS Coordinates: Miles Traveled:

Campground:

Address:

Site:

Check in: Check out: Cost:

☐ Water	☐ Easy Access	☆☆☆☆☆ Location
☐ Sewer	☐ Paved	☆☆☆☆☆ Amenities
☐ Electricity	☐ Restrooms	☆☆☆☆☆ Cleanliness
☐ Wfi	☐ Laundry	☆☆☆☆☆ Security
☐ Fire Ring	☐ Store / Cafe	☆☆☆☆☆ Overall

Pros / Cons:

Notes:

From / To:..

GPS Coordinates:.. Miles Traveled:...............................

Campground:...

Address:..

Site:..

Check in:.............................. Check out:.............................. Cost:...........................

☐ Water	☐ Easy Access	☆☆☆☆☆ Location
☐ Sewer	☐ Paved	☆☆☆☆☆ Amenities
☐ Electricity	☐ Restrooms	☆☆☆☆☆ Cleanliness
☐ Wfi	☐ Laundry	☆☆☆☆☆ Security
☐ Fire Ring	☐ Store / Cafe	☆☆☆☆☆ Overall

Pros / Cons:..

_____

_____

Notes:...

_____

_____

_____

_____

_____

_____

_____

From / To: ....

GPS Coordinates: .... Miles Traveled: ....

Campground: ....

Address: ....

Site: ....

Check in: .... Check out: .... Cost: ....

☐ Water	☐ Easy Access	☆☆☆☆☆ Location
☐ Sewer	☐ Paved	☆☆☆☆☆ Amenities
☐ Electricity	☐ Restrooms	☆☆☆☆☆ Cleanliness
☐ Wfi	☐ Laundry	☆☆☆☆☆ Security
☐ Fire Ring	☐ Store / Cafe	☆☆☆☆☆ Overall

Pros / Cons: ....

....

....

Notes: ....

....

....

....

....

....

....

....

From / To: _____

GPS Coordinates: _____ Miles Traveled: _____

Campground: _____

Address: _____

Site: _____

Check in: _____ Check out: _____ Cost: _____

☐ Water   ☐ Easy Access   ☆☆☆☆☆ Location

☐ Sewer   ☐ Paved   ☆☆☆☆☆ Amenities

☐ Electricity   ☐ Restrooms   ☆☆☆☆☆ Cleanliness

☐ Wfi   ☐ Laundry   ☆☆☆☆☆ Security

☐ Fire Ring   ☐ Store / Cafe   ☆☆☆☆☆ Overall

Pros / Cons: _____

_____

_____

Notes: _____

_____

_____

_____

_____

_____

_____

_____

From / To:..

GPS Coordinates:.. Miles Traveled:............................

Campground:...

Address:..

Site:...

Check in:................................. Check out:................................ Cost:..

☐ Water	☐ Easy Access	☆☆☆☆☆ Location
☐ Sewer	☐ Paved	☆☆☆☆☆ Amenities
☐ Electricity	☐ Restrooms	☆☆☆☆☆ Cleanliness
☐ Wfi	☐ Laundry	☆☆☆☆☆ Security
☐ Fire Ring	☐ Store / Cafe	☆☆☆☆☆ Overall

Pros / Cons:...

_____

_____

Notes:..

_____

_____

_____

_____

_____

_____

_____

_____

From / To:_____

GPS Coordinates:_____ Miles Traveled:_____

Campground:_____

Address:_____

Site:_____

Check in:_____ Check out:_____ Cost:_____

☐ Water	☐ Easy Access	☆☆☆☆☆ Location
☐ Sewer	☐ Paved	☆☆☆☆☆ Amenities
☐ Electricity	☐ Restrooms	☆☆☆☆☆ Cleanliness
☐ Wfi	☐ Laundry	☆☆☆☆☆ Security
☐ Fire Ring	☐ Store / Cafe	☆☆☆☆☆ Overall

Pros / Cons:_____

_____

_____

Notes:_____

_____

_____

_____

_____

_____

_____

_____

From / To: ....

GPS Coordinates: .... Miles Traveled: ....

Campground: ....

Address: ....

Site: ....

Check in: .... Check out: .... Cost: ....

☐ Water   ☐ Easy Access   ☆ ☆ ☆ ☆ ☆   Location

☐ Sewer   ☐ Paved   ☆ ☆ ☆ ☆ ☆   Amenities

☐ Electricity   ☐ Restrooms   ☆ ☆ ☆ ☆ ☆   Cleanliness

☐ Wfi   ☐ Laundry   ☆ ☆ ☆ ☆ ☆   Security

☐ Fire Ring   ☐ Store / Cafe   ☆ ☆ ☆ ☆ ☆   Overall

Pros / Cons: ....

_____

_____

Notes: ....

_____

_____

_____

_____

_____

_____

_____

From / To:_____

GPS Coordinates:_____ Miles Traveled:_____

Campground:_____

Address:_____

Site:_____

Check in:_____ Check out:_____ Cost:_____

☐ Water   ☐ Easy Access   ☆☆☆☆☆ Location
☐ Sewer   ☐ Paved   ☆☆☆☆☆ Amenities
☐ Electricity   ☐ Restrooms   ☆☆☆☆☆ Cleanliness
☐ Wfi   ☐ Laundry   ☆☆☆☆☆ Security
☐ Fire Ring   ☐ Store / Cafe   ☆☆☆☆☆ Overall

Pros / Cons:_____

_____

_____

Notes:_____

_____

_____

_____

_____

_____

_____

_____

From / To:_____

GPS Coordinates:_____ Miles Traveled:_____

Campground:_____

Address:_____

Site:_____

Check in:_____ Check out:_____ Cost:_____

☐ Water	☐ Easy Access	☆ ☆ ☆ ☆ ☆ Location
☐ Sewer	☐ Paved	☆ ☆ ☆ ☆ ☆ Amenities
☐ Electricity	☐ Restrooms	☆ ☆ ☆ ☆ ☆ Cleanliness
☐ Wfi	☐ Laundry	☆ ☆ ☆ ☆ ☆ Security
☐ Fire Ring	☐ Store / Cafe	☆ ☆ ☆ ☆ ☆ Overall

Pros / Cons:_____

_____

_____

Notes:_____

_____

_____

_____

_____

_____

_____

_____

From / To:...

GPS Coordinates:..Miles Traveled:...................

Campground:..

Address:..

Site:..

Check in:................................Check out:...........................Cost:..............

☐ Water   ☐ Easy Access   ☆ ☆ ☆ ☆ ☆ Location

☐ Sewer   ☐ Paved   ☆ ☆ ☆ ☆ ☆ Amenities

☐ Electricity   ☐ Restrooms   ☆ ☆ ☆ ☆ ☆ Cleanliness

☐ Wfi   ☐ Laundry   ☆ ☆ ☆ ☆ ☆ Security

☐ Fire Ring   ☐ Store / Cafe   ☆ ☆ ☆ ☆ ☆ Overall

Pros / Cons:...

_____

_____

Notes:..

_____

_____

_____

_____

_____

_____

_____

From / To:..

GPS Coordinates:..Miles Traveled:..................

Campground:...

Address:...

Site:...

Check in:............................... Check out:............................... Cost:....................

☐ Water	☐ Easy Access	☆☆☆☆☆ Location
☐ Sewer	☐ Paved	☆☆☆☆☆ Amenities
☐ Electricity	☐ Restrooms	☆☆☆☆☆ Cleanliness
☐ Wfi	☐ Laundry	☆☆☆☆☆ Security
☐ Fire Ring	☐ Store / Cafe	☆☆☆☆☆ Overall

Pros / Cons:..

_____

_____

Notes:..

_____

_____

_____

_____

_____

_____

_____

From / To:_____

GPS Coordinates:_____ Miles Traveled:_____

Campground:_____

Address:_____

Site:_____

Check in:_____ Check out:_____ Cost:_____

☐ Water   ☐ Easy Access   ☆ ☆ ☆ ☆ ☆ Location

☐ Sewer   ☐ Paved   ☆ ☆ ☆ ☆ ☆ Amenities

☐ Electricity   ☐ Restrooms   ☆ ☆ ☆ ☆ ☆ Cleanliness

☐ Wfi   ☐ Laundry   ☆ ☆ ☆ ☆ ☆ Security

☐ Fire Ring   ☐ Store / Cafe   ☆ ☆ ☆ ☆ ☆ Overall

Pros / Cons:_____

_____

_____

Notes:_____

_____

_____

_____

_____

_____

_____

_____

From / To:...

GPS Coordinates:..Miles Traveled:.......................................

Campground:..

Address:...

Site:...

Check in:...................................... Check out:............................... Cost:..

☐ Water	☐ Easy Access	☆ ☆ ☆ ☆ ☆ Location
☐ Sewer	☐ Paved	☆ ☆ ☆ ☆ ☆ Amenities
☐ Electricity	☐ Restrooms	☆ ☆ ☆ ☆ ☆ Cleanliness
☐ Wfi	☐ Laundry	☆ ☆ ☆ ☆ ☆ Security
☐ Fire Ring	☐ Store / Cafe	☆ ☆ ☆ ☆ ☆ Overall

Pros / Cons:..

Notes:...

From / To: _____

GPS Coordinates: _____ Miles Traveled: _____

Campground: _____

Address: _____

Site: _____

Check in: _____ Check out: _____ Cost: _____

☐ Water	☐ Easy Access	☆☆☆☆☆ Location
☐ Sewer	☐ Paved	☆☆☆☆☆ Amenities
☐ Electricity	☐ Restrooms	☆☆☆☆☆ Cleanliness
☐ Wfi	☐ Laundry	☆☆☆☆☆ Security
☐ Fire Ring	☐ Store / Cafe	☆☆☆☆☆ Overall

Pros / Cons: _____

_____

_____

Notes: _____

_____

_____

_____

_____

_____

_____

_____

_____

From / To:...

GPS Coordinates:.. Miles Traveled:......................

Campground:...

Address:...

Site:..

Check in:........................... Check out:........................... Cost:..............................

☐ Water	☐ Easy Access	☆ ☆ ☆ ☆ ☆ Location
☐ Sewer	☐ Paved	☆ ☆ ☆ ☆ ☆ Amenities
☐ Electricity	☐ Restrooms	☆ ☆ ☆ ☆ ☆ Cleanliness
☐ Wfi	☐ Laundry	☆ ☆ ☆ ☆ ☆ Security
☐ Fire Ring	☐ Store / Cafe	☆ ☆ ☆ ☆ ☆ Overall

Pros / Cons:...

_____

_____

Notes:...

_____

_____

_____

_____

_____

_____

_____

From / To:..

GPS Coordinates:... Miles Traveled:...........................

Campground:..

Address:..

Site:...

Check in:...................................... Check out:..................................... Cost:............................

☐ Water	☐ Easy Access	☆☆☆☆☆ Location
☐ Sewer	☐ Paved	☆☆☆☆☆ Amenities
☐ Electricity	☐ Restrooms	☆☆☆☆☆ Cleanliness
☐ Wfi	☐ Laundry	☆☆☆☆☆ Security
☐ Fire Ring	☐ Store / Cafe	☆☆☆☆☆ Overall

Pros / Cons:...

Notes:..

From / To:...

GPS Coordinates:... Miles Traveled:.............................

Campground:...

Address:...

Site:...

Check in:................................... Check out:................................... Cost:................................

☐ Water	☐ Easy Access	☆☆☆☆☆ Location
☐ Sewer	☐ Paved	☆☆☆☆☆ Amenities
☐ Electricity	☐ Restrooms	☆☆☆☆☆ Cleanliness
☐ Wfi	☐ Laundry	☆☆☆☆☆ Security
☐ Fire Ring	☐ Store / Cafe	☆☆☆☆☆ Overall

Pros / Cons:...

_____

_____

Notes:...

_____

_____

_____

_____

_____

_____

_____

From / To:..

GPS Coordinates:...Miles Traveled:.............................

Campground:...

Address:..

Site:...

Check in:...........................Check out:...........................Cost:...........................

☐ Water   ☐ Easy Access   ☆☆☆☆☆ Location

☐ Sewer   ☐ Paved   ☆☆☆☆☆ Amenities

☐ Electricity   ☐ Restrooms   ☆☆☆☆☆ Cleanliness

☐ Wfi   ☐ Laundry   ☆☆☆☆☆ Security

☐ Fire Ring   ☐ Store / Cafe   ☆☆☆☆☆ Overall

Pros / Cons:...

....

....

Notes:...

....

....

....

....

....

....

....

From / To:

GPS Coordinates: Miles Traveled:

Campground:

Address:

Site:

Check in: Check out: Cost:

- ☐ Water
- ☐ Sewer
- ☐ Electricity
- ☐ Wfi
- ☐ Fire Ring

- ☐ Easy Access
- ☐ Paved
- ☐ Restrooms
- ☐ Laundry
- ☐ Store / Cafe

☆ ☆ ☆ ☆ ☆ Location

☆ ☆ ☆ ☆ ☆ Amenities

☆ ☆ ☆ ☆ ☆ Cleanliness

☆ ☆ ☆ ☆ ☆ Security

☆ ☆ ☆ ☆ ☆ Overall

Pros / Cons:

Notes:

From / To:

GPS Coordinates: Miles Traveled:

Campground:

Address:

Site:

Check in: Check out: Cost:

☐ Water ☐ Easy Access ☆☆☆☆☆ Location

☐ Sewer ☐ Paved ☆☆☆☆☆ Amenities

☐ Electricity ☐ Restrooms ☆☆☆☆☆ Cleanliness

☐ Wfi ☐ Laundry ☆☆☆☆☆ Security

☐ Fire Ring ☐ Store / Cafe ☆☆☆☆☆ Overall

Pros / Cons:

Notes:

From / To:..

GPS Coordinates:.. Miles Traveled:.......................

Campground:...

Address:...

Site:...

Check in:.......................... Check out:............................... Cost:.......................

☐ Water	☐ Easy Access	☆☆☆☆☆ Location
☐ Sewer	☐ Paved	☆☆☆☆☆ Amenities
☐ Electricity	☐ Restrooms	☆☆☆☆☆ Cleanliness
☐ Wfi	☐ Laundry	☆☆☆☆☆ Security
☐ Fire Ring	☐ Store / Cafe	☆☆☆☆☆ Overall

Pros / Cons:..

Notes:..

From / To:

GPS Coordinates: .... Miles Traveled: ....

Campground:

Address:

Site:

Check in: .... Check out: .... Cost: ....

☐ Water	☐ Easy Access	☆☆☆☆☆ Location
☐ Sewer	☐ Paved	☆☆☆☆☆ Amenities
☐ Electricity	☐ Restrooms	☆☆☆☆☆ Cleanliness
☐ Wfi	☐ Laundry	☆☆☆☆☆ Security
☐ Fire Ring	☐ Store / Cafe	☆☆☆☆☆ Overall

Pros / Cons:

Notes:

From / To:..

GPS Coordinates:.. Miles Traveled:.....................

Campground:...

Address:..

Site:..

Check in:........................... Check out:............................ Cost:..........................

☐ Water   ☐ Easy Access   ☆ ☆ ☆ ☆ ☆ Location

☐ Sewer   ☐ Paved   ☆ ☆ ☆ ☆ ☆ Amenities

☐ Electricity   ☐ Restrooms   ☆ ☆ ☆ ☆ ☆ Cleanliness

☐ Wfi   ☐ Laundry   ☆ ☆ ☆ ☆ ☆ Security

☐ Fire Ring   ☐ Store / Cafe   ☆ ☆ ☆ ☆ ☆ Overall

Pros / Cons:...

_____

_____

Notes:...

_____

_____

_____

_____

_____

_____

_____

From / To:...

GPS Coordinates:...Miles Traveled:....................

Campground:...

Address:...

Site:...

Check in:...........................Check out:..........................Cost:.......................

☐ Water	☐ Easy Access	☆☆☆☆☆ Location
☐ Sewer	☐ Paved	☆☆☆☆☆ Amenities
☐ Electricity	☐ Restrooms	☆☆☆☆☆ Cleanliness
☐ Wfi	☐ Laundry	☆☆☆☆☆ Security
☐ Fire Ring	☐ Store / Cafe	☆☆☆☆☆ Overall

Pros / Cons:..

_____

_____

Notes:...

_____

_____

_____

_____

_____

_____

From / To:...

GPS Coordinates:..Miles Traveled:..........................

Campground:..

Address:...

Site:...

Check in:.............................Check out:.............................Cost:.............................

☐ Water	☐ Easy Access	☆☆☆☆☆ Location
☐ Sewer	☐ Paved	☆☆☆☆☆ Amenities
☐ Electricity	☐ Restrooms	☆☆☆☆☆ Cleanliness
☐ Wfi	☐ Laundry	☆☆☆☆☆ Security
☐ Fire Ring	☐ Store / Cafe	☆☆☆☆☆ Overall

Pros / Cons:...

....

....

Notes:...

....

....

....

....

....

....

....

From / To:...

GPS Coordinates:..Miles Traveled:......................................

Campground:...

Address:..

Site:...

Check in:..............................Check out:...............................Cost:..

- [ ] Water
- [ ] Sewer
- [ ] Electricity
- [ ] Wfi
- [ ] Fire Ring

- [ ] Easy Access
- [ ] Paved
- [ ] Restrooms
- [ ] Laundry
- [ ] Store / Cafe

☆ ☆ ☆ ☆ ☆ Location
☆ ☆ ☆ ☆ ☆ Amenities
☆ ☆ ☆ ☆ ☆ Cleanliness
☆ ☆ ☆ ☆ ☆ Security
☆ ☆ ☆ ☆ ☆ Overall

Pros / Cons:...

Notes:...

From / To:..

GPS Coordinates:... Miles Traveled:..................

Campground:...

Address:..

Site:...

Check in:.............................. Check out:.............................. Cost:.....................

☐ Water	☐ Easy Access	☆☆☆☆☆ Location
☐ Sewer	☐ Paved	☆☆☆☆☆ Amenities
☐ Electricity	☐ Restrooms	☆☆☆☆☆ Cleanliness
☐ Wfi	☐ Laundry	☆☆☆☆☆ Security
☐ Fire Ring	☐ Store / Cafe	☆☆☆☆☆ Overall

Pros / Cons:...

Notes:...

Made in the USA
Las Vegas, NV
18 July 2023

74947624R00073